Journey Into Nature

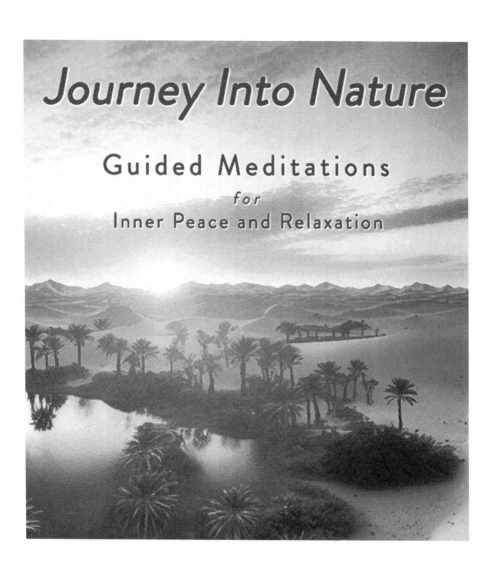

Journey Into Nature

Guided Meditations
for
Inner Peace and Relaxation

Asheville Bellingham Ithaca

Journey Into Nature:
Guided Meditations for Inner Peace and Relaxation

Copyright © 2024 by The Playhard Project

Published by The Playhard Press
The Playhard Press is an imprint of The Playhard Project LLC.

Matthew Barrington, Managing Director
Margaret Ellis, Script Editor
Steven B. Dodson, Operations Consultant
ManeStage Media, Media Consultant

All Rights Reserved. No part of this publication may be reproduced, stored in a retrieval system, or transmitted in any form or by any means, electronic, mechanical, photocopying, recording, or otherwise, without written permission of the publisher.

This book is a work of fiction. Names, characters, places, and incidents are either the product of the author's imagination or are used fictitiously, and any resemblance to actual persons, living or dead, business establishments, events, or locales is entirely coincidental.

playhardpress.com
playhardproject.com

ISBN 978-1-954305-21-2

Dedication

To Wylder

Table of Contents

Introduction...1

Forest Sanctuary..9

Take your listeners on a journey through a peaceful forest, where they can imagine the gentle rustle of leaves, the scent of pine trees, and the warmth of dappled sunlight filtering through the canopy. Encourage them to explore this tranquil sanctuary, finding a sense of calm and renewal amidst the natural beauty.

Lakeside Retreat..16

Transport your listeners to the edge of a serene lake, where they can visualize the stillness of the water, the gentle lapping of waves against the shore, and the chorus of birdsong in the surrounding trees. Invite them to imagine themselves sitting beside the lake, feeling a deep sense of relaxation and contentment.

Mountain Peak Meditation..............................23

Guide your listeners on a journey to the summit of a majestic mountain, where they can envision the expansive views stretching out before them, the crisp mountain air filling their lungs, and the sense of accomplishment and awe at reaching such heights. Encourage them to connect with their inner strength and resilience as they stand atop the world.

Beachside Bliss...30

Lead your listeners to a pristine beach, where they can imagine the feel of warm sand beneath their feet, the sound of waves crashing against the shore, and the salty tang of ocean breeze on their skin. Encourage them to let go of stress and tension as they soak up the tranquil beauty of the beach.

Mountain Meadow...37

Take your listeners on a journey to a serene meadow nestled among the mountains. They can imagine the vibrant colors of wildflowers, the gentle breeze rustling through the grass, and the panoramic views of snow-capped peaks in the distance. This theme could evoke a sense of peace, tranquility, and connection to the beauty of the natural world.

Tropical Rainforest..45

Transport your listeners to the lush, vibrant world of a tropical rainforest. They can visualize towering trees, exotic plants, and cascading waterfalls, while listening to the sounds of chirping birds, buzzing insects, and trickling streams. This theme could offer a sense of adventure, exploration, and awe at the richness of biodiversity.

Desert Oasis 54

Guide your listeners to an oasis in the midst of a vast desert landscape. They can imagine the cool shade of palm trees, the refreshing taste of clear water, and the golden hues of sand stretching out to the horizon. This theme could evoke a feeling of rejuvenation, renewal, and resilience in the face of adversity.

Enchanted Forest 62

Lead your listeners into a mystical forest filled with ancient trees, winding pathways, and hidden glades. They can imagine the soft glow of fireflies, the mysterious rustle of unseen creatures, and the sense of wonder at encountering magical realms. This theme could inspire a sense of curiosity, imagination, and wonderment.

Mountain Lake..69

Guide your listeners to a tranquil lake nestled among towering mountains. They can visualize the mirror-like surface of the water, the majestic peaks reflected in its depths, and the peaceful solitude of the surrounding wilderness. This theme could evoke a sense of serenity, reflection, and connection to the beauty of nature.

Canyon Serenity..78

Take your listeners on a journey into the heart of a majestic canyon, where towering cliffs rise up on either side, and a gentle river winds its way through the rocky landscape. Encourage them to visualize the play of light and shadow on the canyon walls, the soothing sound of water echoing off the rocks, and the feeling of awe and wonder at the grandeur of nature.

Mystical Cavern..85

Lead your listeners into the depths of a hidden cavern, where stalactites hang like icicles from the ceiling, and crystal-clear pools reflect the shimmering glow of bioluminescent life. Invite them to imagine the cool, damp air on their skin, the echo of their footsteps as they explore the cavern, and the sense of mystery and magic that permeates the ancient stone walls.

Arctic Tundra..92

Transport your listeners to a vast, frozen landscape where the tundra stretches out as far as the eye can see, dotted with hardy shrubs, lichen-covered rocks, and patches of colorful wildflowers. Encourage them to visualize the endless expanse of snow and ice, the crisp, clean air filling their lungs, and the silence broken only by the occasional call of a distant bird or the howl of a passing wolf.

Sunset Overlook..99

Guide your listeners to a breathtaking overlook where they can watch the sun dip below the horizon, painting the sky with a symphony of vibrant colors. Invite them to imagine the warm glow of the fading sunlight on their skin, the gentle breeze ruffling their hair, and the feeling of peace and contentment that comes from witnessing the beauty of a sunset in nature.

Celestial Observatory..................................105

Lead your listeners to a secluded observatory nestled high in the mountains, where they can gaze up at the starry expanse of the night sky and marvel at the wonders of the universe. Encourage them to visualize the twinkling stars overhead, the soft whisper of the wind in the trees, and the sense of wonder and awe at the vastness of space and time.

Conclusion...111

Introduction

Embarking on a Journey of Transformation with Guided Imagery Meditation

Welcome to "Journey Into Nature: Guided Meditations for Inner Peace and Relaxation," a collection designed to transport you to serene landscapes, tranquil retreats, and mystical realms through the power of visualization. Guided imagery is a therapeutic technique that harnesses the innate connection between the mind and body to promote healing, relaxation, and well-being. In this introduction, we'll explore the benefits of guided imagery, the science behind its effectiveness, and practical tips for using guided imagery scripts to enhance mental and emotional health.

The Benefits of Guided Imagery

Guided imagery has been used for centuries as a tool for healing and self-discovery, with a wealth of research supporting its effectiveness for a wide range of health conditions. Scientific studies have shown that guided imagery can reduce stress, anxiety, and depression, improve sleep quality, and enhance overall well-being. By engaging the imagination and activating the body's relaxation response, guided imagery promotes a sense of calm and inner peace, allowing individuals to tap into their natural healing abilities and find relief from physical and emotional discomfort.

The Science Behind Guided Imagery

At the heart of guided imagery is the principle of neuroplasticity—the brain's ability to reorganize itself in response to new experiences and stimuli. When we engage in guided imagery, we activate specific neural pathways associated with relaxation, creativity, and emotional regulation, leading to measurable changes in brain activity and physiological responses. Through vivid visualization and sensory engagement, guided imagery stimulates the release of neurotransmitters and hormones that promote relaxation and well-being, creating a cascade of positive effects throughout the body and mind.

Versatility of Guided Imagery

One of the most remarkable aspects of guided imagery is its versatility as a therapeutic tool. From reducing pain and discomfort to enhancing creativity and performance, guided imagery can be adapted to address a wide range of health goals and concerns. Whether you're seeking relief from chronic pain, coping with stress and anxiety, or simply looking to deepen your connection to yourself and the world around you, guided imagery offers a pathway to healing and transformation that is accessible to people of all ages, backgrounds, and abilities.

Practical Guidance for Practitioners

As you guide others through the transformative experience of guided imagery, here are six practical tips to enhance your delivery and facilitate a deep and meaningful experience:

1. **Create a Calm and Comfortable Environment**
   Before beginning the guided imagery session, ensure that the environment is conducive to relaxation and focused attention. Dim the lights,

eliminate distractions, and encourage participants to find a comfortable seated or reclined position.

2 Set the Stage for Relaxation

As you introduce the guided imagery script, use a soothing and reassuring tone of voice to help participants feel at ease and receptive to the experience. Encourage them to take several deep breaths and let go of any tension or stress they may be holding onto.

3 Engage the Senses

Throughout the guided imagery session, the participants' senses will be engaged through the use of descriptive language and imagery that evokes vivid sensory experiences. Encourage them to visualize the scenery, feel the sensations in their bodies, and listen to the sounds of nature as if they were actually there.

4 Encourage Mindfulness and Presence

Remind participants to stay present in the moment and to allow themselves to fully immerse in the guided imagery experience. Encourage them to let go of any distracting thoughts or concerns and to focus their attention on the sensations and imagery unfolding in their minds.

5 Trust the Process

Trust in the power of the guided imagery script to guide participants on their journey of relaxation and self-discovery. Allow pauses for reflection and contemplation, and give participants the space they need to explore their inner landscape at their own pace.

6 Facilitate Post-Session Reflection

After completing the guided imagery session, invite participants to share their experiences and insights if they feel comfortable doing so. Encourage them to take a few moments to reflect on how they feel and to notice any changes in their mood, energy, or state of mind.

As a practitioner of guided imagery, you have the power to facilitate profound healing and transformation in the lives of others. By following these practical guidance tips and embracing the role of guide and facilitator, you can create a safe and supportive space for participants to explore their inner landscape, nurture their well-being, and cultivate a deeper connection to themselves and the world around them.

Final Thoughts

As you embark on your journey into the world of guided imagery, may you discover the transformative power of visualization and the profound connection between mind, body, and spirit. Visualizing serene and beautiful landscapes can lead to deep relaxation, reducing the stress and anxiety that often burden our daily lives. Each script in this collection is designed to help you tap into your inner reservoir of peace and tranquility, allowing you to find moments of calm amidst the chaos. As you continue to explore the power of guided imagery, you'll find that these journeys not only soothe the mind but also promote a harmonious balance between your physical and spiritual selves. Use these scripts to inspire creativity, foster inner peace, and cultivate a deeper connection to the world around you. May they help you unlock the full potential of your mind's eye and lead you toward a more mindful and fulfilling life.

Forest Sanctuary

Welcome to your Forest Sanctuary, a haven of peace and tranquility nestled deep within the embrace of nature. Find a comfortable position, either sitting or lying down, and gently close your eyes. Take a deep breath in through your nose, allowing the cool, clean air to fill your lungs, and exhale slowly through your mouth, releasing any tension or stress you may be holding onto.

As you begin your journey, visualize yourself standing at the edge of a vast and verdant forest. Take a moment to observe the towering trees that surround you, their sturdy trunks rising up like ancient pillars, their branches reaching towards the sky in a canopy of greenery. Feel the soft earth beneath your feet, alive with the rich tapestry of life that thrives in this tranquil sanctuary.

Now, let's engage your senses fully as you immerse yourself in the beauty of the forest. Listen closely to the symphony of nature that surrounds you—the gentle rustle of leaves as they sway in the breeze, the melodic chirping of birds as they flit from branch to branch, the soothing murmur of a nearby stream as it winds its way through the underbrush.

Take a deep breath in and inhale the earthy aroma of the forest—the scent of damp soil and decaying leaves, the sweet perfume of wildflowers blooming in the dappled sunlight. Let the fragrance fill your senses, grounding you in the present moment and awakening a deep connection to the natural world around you.

Feel the warmth of the sun on your skin, filtered through the dense canopy overhead. Close your eyes and bask in its golden glow, allowing its radiant energy to penetrate deep into your bones, filling you with a sense of warmth and vitality.

As you begin to explore the forest, notice the intricate details of your surroundings—the delicate ferns unfurling in the shade, the vibrant hues of wildflowers carpeting the forest floor, the rough texture of tree bark beneath your fingertips. Take your time as you meander along winding pathways, allowing yourself to be fully present in each moment.

Perhaps you come across a babbling brook, its crystal-clear waters glistening in the sunlight. Sit down beside it and dip your fingers into the cool stream, feeling the gentle rush of water against your skin. Listen to the soothing sound of the flowing water as it washes away any lingering tension or stress, leaving you feeling refreshed and renewed.

Or maybe you stumble upon a secluded glade, a hidden sanctuary untouched by the outside world. Lie down amidst the soft grass and gaze up at the patchwork of sunlight filtering through the leaves above. Watch as the leaves dance and sway in the breeze, casting ever-changing patterns of light and shadow on the forest floor.

Take a few moments to simply be, allowing yourself to surrender to the natural rhythms of the forest. Feel the gentle rise and fall of your chest as you breathe in time with the earth, becoming one with the pulse of life that courses through the forest.

End ⟶ Know that you can return to this sacred sanctuary whenever you need to find peace and solace amidst the chaos of daily life. When you're ready, slowly begin to bring your awareness back to the present moment, carrying with you the sense of calm and renewal that you've discovered here. Open your eyes, feeling refreshed and rejuvenated, and take a moment to express gratitude for the beauty and wonder of the natural world. ■

or

Extend

⬇ As you continue your journey through the forest, allow yourself to sink deeper into a state of relaxation and tranquility. Notice the interplay of light and shadow as the sun filters through the dense canopy above, creating a mosaic of patterns on the forest floor. Take a moment to appreciate the beauty of this natural masterpiece, a testament to the intricate balance of life and energy that permeates the forest.

With each step you take, feel your connection to the earth strengthening beneath your feet. Imagine roots extending from the soles of your feet, anchoring you firmly to the ground below. Feel the steady pulse of the earth beneath you, a constant reminder of the profound interconnectedness of all living beings.

As you walk, allow your senses to guide you deeper into the heart of the forest. Notice the subtle changes in temperature as you move from sunlight into shade, the coolness of the breeze as it caresses your skin, the symphony of sounds that surrounds you—birds singing, leaves rustling, water flowing—all blending together in a harmonious chorus of life.

Take a moment to pause and admire the majestic trees that tower above you, their branches reaching towards the sky like outstretched arms. Feel a sense of awe and reverence for these ancient guardians of the forest, standing tall and proud against the passage of time.

As you continue your journey, you may come across a clearing bathed in sunlight, a sacred space where time seems to stand still. Sit down amidst the soft grass and close your eyes, allowing yourself to be fully present in this moment of stillness and serenity.

Take a deep breath in and let the sweet scent of wildflowers fill your nostrils, their delicate fragrance mingling with the earthy aroma of the forest. Feel a sense of peace wash over you as you surrender to the beauty and tranquility of this sacred sanctuary.

As you sit, take a moment to reflect on the abundance of life that surrounds you—the intricate web of interconnectedness that binds all living beings together in a delicate tapestry of existence. Feel a sense of gratitude welling up within you for the gift of life and the opportunity to experience the wonders of the natural world.

In this moment of quiet contemplation, allow yourself to release any lingering tension or stress that you may be carrying. Feel it melting away with each exhale, leaving you feeling lighter, freer, and more at peace with yourself and the world around you.

Know that you can return to this forest sanctuary whenever you need to find solace and renewal amidst the chaos of daily life. Carry the sense of peace and tranquility that you've discovered here with you as you journey forward, knowing that you are always connected to the beauty and wisdom of the natural world.

When you're ready, slowly begin to bring your awareness back to the present moment, gently opening your eyes and taking a few deep breaths. Take a moment to stretch your limbs and wiggle your fingers and toes, feeling the energy flowing freely through your body once more.

Lakeside Retreat

Welcome to your Lakeside Retreat, a tranquil oasis of peace and serenity nestled on the edge of a serene lake. Find a comfortable position, either sitting or lying down, and gently close your eyes. Take a deep breath in through your nose, allowing the fresh, clean air to fill your lungs, and exhale slowly through your mouth, releasing any tension or stress you may be holding onto.

As you begin your journey, imagine yourself standing on the shore of a beautiful lake, its surface calm and still, reflecting the clear blue sky above like a mirror. Take a moment to soak in the breathtaking beauty of your surroundings—the tranquil water stretching out before you, the lush greenery of the surrounding landscape, the gentle rustle of leaves in the breeze.

Now, let's engage your senses fully as you immerse yourself in the peace and tranquility of this lakeside retreat. Close your eyes and listen closely to the sounds of nature that surround you—the gentle lapping of waves against the shore, the chorus of birdsong echoing through the trees, the distant hum of insects in the air.

As you listen, feel a sense of calm and contentment washing over you, like a warm embrace from the natural world. Allow yourself to be fully present in this moment, letting go of any worries or distractions as you surrender to the beauty and serenity of the lake.

Take a deep breath in and inhale the crisp, clean scent of the lake—the earthy aroma of wet sand, the tangy scent of fresh water, the sweet fragrance of wildflowers blooming along the shore. Let the scent fill your nostrils, invigorating your senses and grounding you in the present moment.

Feel the warmth of the sun on your skin as you imagine yourself sitting beside the lake, basking in its golden rays. Feel the soft, cool sand beneath your feet, the gentle breeze ruffling your hair, the warmth of the sun kissing your skin. Allow yourself to relax completely, sinking into a state of deep relaxation and contentment.

As you sit by the lake, take a moment to observe the beauty of your surroundings—the shimmering surface of the water, the graceful movement of the reeds swaying in the breeze, the playful dance of sunlight on the waves. Let yourself be mesmerized by the ever-changing patterns and colors, finding peace and joy in the simple beauty of nature.

Dip your toes into the cool, refreshing water of the lake, feeling its soothing embrace enveloping you like a gentle caress. Taste the clean, pure water on your lips, savoring its crisp, refreshing flavor as it quenches your thirst and nourishes your body.

Take a few moments to simply be, allowing yourself to connect with the natural rhythms of the lake and the surrounding landscape. Feel a sense of gratitude welling up within you for the gift of this moment, for the opportunity to experience the wonder and beauty of the natural world.

End ⟶ Know that you can return to this lakeside retreat whenever you need to find peace and solace amidst the chaos of daily life. Carry the sense of calm and contentment that you've discovered here with you as you journey forward, knowing that you are always connected to the healing power of nature.

or

Extend

When you're ready, slowly begin to bring your awareness back to the present moment, gently opening your eyes and taking a few deep breaths. Take a moment to stretch your limbs and wiggle your fingers and toes, feeling the energy flowing freely through your body once more. ■

As you continue to sit by the lake, allow yourself to become fully immersed in the sights and sounds of this serene oasis. Notice the gentle ripples on the surface of the water, shimmering in the sunlight like a sea of diamonds. Watch as a family of ducks glides gracefully across the lake, leaving a trail of tiny waves in their wake.

Listen to the symphony of nature that surrounds you—the gentle lapping of waves, the rustling of leaves in the breeze, the melodic chirping of birds. Each sound blends seamlessly together, creating a soothing soundtrack that lulls you into a state of deep relaxation.

As you gaze out across the lake, let your eyes wander to the distant shore, where tall trees stand towering to the sky. Imagine yourself on the other side, exploring the dense forest, discovering hidden treasures and secret pathways as you wander through this enchanted realm.

Feel a sense of wonder and awe as you observe the intricate dance of life unfolding around you. Notice the delicate balance of ecosystems, the interdependence of plants and animals, and the profound beauty of the natural world. Allow yourself to feel a deep connection to all living beings, knowing that you are a part of this vast and interconnected web of life.

Take a deep breath in and inhale the pure, fresh air of the lake. Feel it filling your lungs, energizing your body, and rejuvenating your spirit. With each breath, feel a sense of clarity and peace washing over you, clearing away any lingering stress or negativity.

As you sit by the lake, take a moment to reflect on the beauty and wonder of nature. Consider the lessons that the lake has to offer—the importance of stillness and reflection, the power of resilience and adaptability, the beauty of simplicity and harmony.

In this moment of quiet contemplation, allow yourself to release any burdens or worries that you may be carrying. Let them float away on the gentle breeze, leaving you feeling lighter, freer, and more at peace with yourself and the world around you.

Know that you can return to this lakeside retreat whenever you need to find solace and renewal. Carry the sense of calm and contentment that you've discovered here with you as you journey forward, knowing that you are always connected to the healing power of nature.

When you're ready, slowly begin to bring your awareness back to the present moment, gently opening your eyes and taking a few deep breaths. Take a moment to stretch your limbs and wiggle your fingers and toes, feeling the energy flowing freely through your body once more.

Mountain Peak Meditation

Welcome to your Mountain Peak Meditation, a journey to the summit of a majestic mountain where you can connect with your inner strength and resilience. Find a comfortable position, either sitting or lying down, and gently close your eyes. Take a deep breath in through your nose, feeling the crisp mountain air fill your lungs, and exhale slowly through your mouth, releasing any tension or stress you may be holding onto.

As you begin your ascent, imagine yourself standing at the base of a towering mountain, its peak obscured by swirling clouds. Feel the solid earth beneath your feet, the rough texture of the rocks beneath your hands, as you prepare to embark on this epic journey.

With each step you take, feel your determination and resolve growing stronger within you. Visualize the winding path stretching out before you, leading ever upwards towards the summit. Take a moment to appreciate the beauty of your surroundings—the rugged cliffs, the lush valleys, the vibrant wildflowers that dot the landscape.

Now, let's engage your senses fully as you ascend the mountain. Close your eyes and listen closely to the sounds of nature that surround you—the distant cry of a soaring eagle, the rustling of leaves in the breeze, the gentle rush of a nearby stream. Allow these sounds to guide you forward, filling you with a sense of purpose and determination.

As you climb higher, feel the temperature dropping, the air growing cooler and crisper with each passing moment. Inhale deeply and breathe in the clean, invigorating scent of the mountain air—the scent of pine trees, the tang of distant snow, the faint aroma of wild herbs clinging to the breeze.

Feel the sensation of exertion in your muscles as you climb, the burn of exertion mingling with the exhilaration of progress. Feel your heart beating steadily in your chest, a rhythmic reminder of your body's strength and vitality.

As you continue your ascent, visualize the expansive views stretching out before you—the sweeping vistas, the jagged peaks, the endless expanse of sky. Allow yourself to be awed by the sheer magnitude of the landscape, feeling a sense of wonder and reverence for the natural world.

With each step you take, feel yourself drawing closer to the summit, your determination driving you forward even as your body grows tired. Visualize the final push to the top, the exhilaration of reaching such heights, the sense of accomplishment and awe as you stand atop the world.

As you reach the summit, take a moment to pause and appreciate the beauty of your surroundings. Look out across the landscape, feeling a deep sense of peace and contentment wash over you. Take a deep breath in and inhale the pure, crisp air of the mountain peak, savoring its invigorating taste on your tongue.

Take a few moments to simply be, allowing yourself to connect with the vastness and majesty of the natural world. Feel a sense of gratitude welling up within you for the opportunity to experience such beauty and wonder.

End ⟶ Know that you can return to this mountain peak meditation whenever you need to find strength and resilience within yourself. Carry the sense of accomplishment and awe that you've discovered here with you as you journey forward, knowing that you are capable of overcoming any obstacle that comes your way.

or

Extend

When you're ready, slowly begin to bring your awareness back to the present moment, gently opening your eyes and taking a few deep breaths. Take a moment to stretch your limbs and wiggle your fingers and toes, feeling the energy flowing freely through your body once more. ∎

As you stand atop the mountain peak, take a moment to soak in the breathtaking beauty of your surroundings. Feel the cool mountain breeze brushing against your skin, refreshing and invigorating as it whispers through the peaks and valleys.

With each breath you take, feel a sense of peace and clarity washing over you, clearing away any lingering doubts or fears. Allow yourself to be fully present in this moment, embracing the profound sense of freedom and possibility that comes from standing atop the world.

Now, let's engage your senses fully as you connect with the natural beauty of the mountain peak. Close your eyes and listen closely to the sounds of the wilderness—the gentle rustle of leaves in the wind, the distant call of a soaring eagle, the rhythmic beat of your own heart. Let these sounds envelop you, filling you with a sense of calm and serenity.

As you listen, feel the warmth of the sun on your skin, its golden rays casting a soft glow over the landscape. Visualize the vibrant colors of the mountainside—the deep greens of the forests, the shimmering blues of the lakes, the fiery oranges and reds of the autumn foliage. Allow yourself to be mesmerized by the ever-changing palette of nature, finding beauty and wonder in every hue.

With each step you take, feel the solid earth beneath your feet, grounding you in the present moment. Reach out and touch the rough texture of the rocks, the smooth bark of the trees, the softness of the wildflowers that carpet the ground. Let yourself be fully immersed in the tactile sensations of the mountain, feeling a deep connection to the natural world around you.

As you explore the summit, take a moment to savor the taste of adventure on your lips. Imagine the tang of fresh mountain air, the sweetness of wild berries plucked from the bushes, the crispness of snowflakes melting on your tongue. Let each flavor awaken your senses, filling you with a sense of vitality and exploration.

Take a few moments to simply be, allowing yourself to soak in the peace and tranquility of the mountain peak. Feel a sense of gratitude welling up within you for the opportunity to experience such beauty and wonder. Know that you can return to this mountain peak meditation whenever you need to find strength and resilience within yourself.

Carry the sense of accomplishment and awe that you've discovered here with you as you journey forward, knowing that you are capable of overcoming any obstacle that comes your way. When you're ready, slowly begin to bring your awareness back to the present moment, gently opening your eyes and taking a few deep breaths.

Beachside Bliss

Welcome to your Beachside Bliss meditation, a journey to a pristine beach where you can let go of stress and tension and immerse yourself in the tranquil beauty of the ocean. Find a comfortable position, either sitting or lying down, and gently close your eyes. Take a deep breath in through your nose, allowing the salty tang of ocean breeze to fill your lungs, and exhale slowly through your mouth, releasing any tension or stress you may be holding onto.

As you begin your journey, imagine yourself standing on the shore of a pristine beach, the soft sand warm beneath your feet, the gentle sound of waves lapping at the shore filling your ears. Take a moment to visualize the expansive stretch of coastline before you, the endless expanse of sparkling blue water stretching out to the horizon.

Now, let's engage your senses fully as you immerse yourself in the beauty of the beach. Close your eyes and listen closely to the sounds of the ocean—the rhythmic crash of waves against the shore, the distant cry of seagulls soaring overhead, the soothing hum of the breeze as it rustles through the palm trees. Let these sounds wash over you, filling you with a sense of peace and tranquility.

As you listen, feel the warmth of the sun on your skin, its golden rays kissing your face and shoulders, filling you with a sense of warmth and vitality. Visualize the vibrant colors of the beach—the powdery white sand, the crystal-clear water, the lush green palm trees swaying gently in the breeze. Allow yourself to be mesmerized by the beauty of your surroundings, finding peace and serenity in the simplicity of nature.

With each breath you take, feel the cool, salty breeze brushing against your skin, refreshing and invigorating as it caresses your cheeks and ruffles your hair. Inhale deeply and breathe in the clean, briny scent of the ocean—the scent of saltwater and seaweed, the tang of sunscreen and coconut oil, the faint aroma of tropical flowers blooming nearby. Let these scents transport you to a place of pure relaxation and bliss.

As you walk along the shoreline, feel the soft sand shifting beneath your feet, molding to the contours of your soles with each step you take. Reach out and touch the cool, wet sand, the gentle lapping of waves washing over your toes, the smooth texture of seashells scattered along the shore. Let yourself be fully immersed in the tactile sensations of the beach, feeling a deep connection to the natural world around you.

Take a few moments to simply be, allowing yourself to soak in the tranquil beauty of the beach. Feel a sense of gratitude welling up within you for the opportunity to experience such peace and serenity. Know that you can return to this beachside bliss whenever you need to find solace and renewal.

End ⟶ Carry the sense of relaxation and
or tranquility that you've discovered here with
Extend you as you journey forward, knowing that
you are always connected to the healing
power of nature. When you're ready, slowly
begin to bring your awareness back to the
present moment, gently opening your eyes
and taking a few deep breaths. Take a
moment to stretch your limbs and wiggle
your fingers and toes, feeling the energy
flowing freely through your body once
more. ■

As you stand on the shore of this pristine beach, take a moment to feel the gentle rhythm of the waves washing over you, grounding you in the present moment. With each wave that rolls in, imagine it carrying away any stress or tension you may be holding onto, leaving you feeling lighter and more at peace with yourself and the world.

Now, let's engage your senses fully as you continue to immerse yourself in the beauty of the beach. With the full power of your imagination, listen closely to the sounds of the ocean—the soothing rhythm of waves crashing against the shore, the playful chatter of seabirds circling overhead, the distant murmur of voices carried on the breeze. Let these sounds wash over you, filling you with a sense of calm and tranquility.

As you listen, feel the warmth of the sun on your skin, its gentle caress enveloping you like a comforting embrace. Visualize the vibrant colors of the beach—the soft golden sand, the sparkling turquoise water, the vivid hues of tropical flowers blooming along the shoreline. Allow yourself to be enchanted by the beauty of your surroundings, finding joy and serenity in the simple pleasures of nature.

With each breath you take, feel the cool, salty breeze blowing through your hair, invigorating and refreshing as it fills your lungs with clean, briny air. Inhale deeply and breathe in the salty tang of the ocean—the scent of seawater and sunscreen, the earthy aroma of driftwood and seaweed, the faint hint of tropical fruits carried on the breeze. Let these scents transport you to a place of pure relaxation and bliss.

As you stroll along the water's edge, feel the soft sand beneath your feet, the gentle pressure of each step sinking into the cool, wet sand. Reach down and scoop up a handful of sand, letting it trickle through your fingers like grains of time slipping away. Feel a sense of connection to the earth beneath your feet, a reminder of your place in the natural world.

Take a moment to pause and gaze out at the vast expanse of the ocean before you, feeling a sense of wonder and awe at its boundless beauty and power. Watch as the sunlight dances across the water, casting shimmering reflections that stretch out to the horizon. Allow yourself to be filled with a deep sense of gratitude for the opportunity to experience such magnificence.

Know that you can return to this beachside bliss whenever you need to find peace and serenity amidst the chaos of daily life. Carry the sense of relaxation and tranquility that you've discovered here with you as you journey forward, knowing that you are always connected to the healing power of nature.

    When you're ready, slowly begin to bring your awareness back to the present moment, gently opening your eyes and taking a few deep breaths. Take a moment to stretch your limbs and wiggle your fingers and toes, feeling the energy flowing freely through your body once more.

Mountain Meadow

Welcome to your Mountain Meadow meditation, a journey to a serene meadow nestled among the mountains where you can connect with the beauty and tranquility of the natural world. Find a comfortable position, either sitting or lying down, and gently close your eyes. Take a deep breath in through your nose, allowing the fresh mountain air to fill your lungs, and exhale slowly through your mouth, releasing any tension or stress you may be holding onto.

As you begin your journey, imagine yourself standing on the edge of a lush mountain meadow, the vibrant colors of wildflowers painting the landscape in hues of red, yellow, purple, and blue. Take a moment to visualize the panoramic views stretching out before you—the rugged peaks of the mountains rising majestically in the distance, their snow-capped summits glistening in the sunlight.

Now, let's engage your senses fully as you immerse yourself in the beauty of the mountain meadow. Close your eyes and listen closely to the sounds of nature—the gentle rustle of grass in the breeze, the melodic chirping of birdsong echoing through the valley, the distant rush of a mountain stream cascading down the rocky slopes. Let these sounds envelop you, filling you with a sense of peace and tranquility.

As you listen, feel the warmth of the sun on your skin, its golden rays dancing across your face and arms, filling you with a sense of warmth and vitality. Visualize the vibrant colors of the meadow—the soft green grass, the brilliant hues of wildflowers swaying in the breeze, the deep blue sky stretching out overhead. Allow yourself to be mesmerized by the beauty of your surroundings, finding peace and serenity in the simplicity of nature.

With each breath you take, feel the cool, crisp mountain air filling your lungs, invigorating and refreshing as it cleanses your body and mind. Inhale deeply and breathe in the clean, earthy scent of the meadow—the aroma of wildflowers and grasses, the piney fragrance of evergreen trees, the faint hint of mountain herbs carried on the breeze. Let these scents transport you to a place of pure relaxation and bliss.

As you walk through the meadow, feel the soft grass beneath your feet, the gentle pressure of each step sinking into the earth. Reach out and touch the delicate petals of a wildflower, the smooth texture of its petals brushing against your fingertips, the fragrant scent rising up to greet you. Let yourself be fully immersed in the tactile sensations of the meadow, feeling a deep connection to the natural world around you.

Take a moment to pause and gaze out at the majestic mountains surrounding the meadow, feeling a sense of awe and wonder at their towering beauty. Watch as the sunlight dances across the peaks, casting ever-changing patterns of light and shadow on the landscape below. Allow yourself to be filled with a deep sense of gratitude for the opportunity to experience such magnificence.

End ⟶ Know that you can return to this mountain meadow whenever you need to find peace and serenity amidst the chaos of daily life. Carry the sense of relaxation and tranquility that you've discovered here with you as you journey forward, knowing that you are always connected to the healing power of nature.

or

Extend

When you're ready, slowly begin to bring your awareness back to the present moment, gently opening your eyes and taking a few deep breaths. Take a moment to stretch your limbs and wiggle your fingers and toes, feeling the energy flowing freely through your body once more. ■

↓ As you stand in the midst of the mountain meadow, take a moment to fully immerse yourself in the beauty and tranquility that surrounds you. Feel the gentle breeze rustling through the grass, lifting your hair and carrying with it the sweet scent of wildflowers and pine trees. With each inhale, feel a sense of invigoration and renewal filling your lungs, revitalizing your body and mind.

Now, let's deepen your connection to this serene landscape by engaging your senses even further. Close your eyes once more and listen closely to the sounds of the meadow—the soft chirping of crickets hidden in the grass, the gentle hum of bees buzzing from flower to flower, the distant call of a bird soaring overhead. Let these sounds wash over you, enveloping you in a symphony of nature's melody.

As you listen, feel the warmth of the sun on your skin, its rays dancing across your face and shoulders, filling you with a sense of warmth and comfort. Visualize the vibrant colors of the meadow—the rich greens of the grass, the vivid hues of the wildflowers, the deep blues of the sky above. Allow yourself to be captivated by the beauty of your surroundings, finding peace and serenity in the ever-changing landscape.

With each breath you take, feel the earth beneath your feet, solid and grounding, supporting you as you stand amidst the beauty of the mountain meadow. Reach out and touch the rough bark of a nearby tree, the smooth leaves of a blooming vine, the cool surface of a stone slowly being warmed by the sun. Let yourself be fully present in this moment, feeling a deep connection to the natural world around you.

Take a moment to pause and gaze out at the panoramic views of the surrounding mountains, their snow-capped peaks rising majestically against the clear blue sky. Marvel at the sheer scale and grandeur of these ancient giants, feeling a sense of awe and reverence for the forces of nature that have shaped them over millennia.

As you continue to explore the meadow, allow yourself to be guided by your intuition, following the path that calls to you. Perhaps you come across a tranquil stream, its crystal-clear waters winding their way through the landscape like a ribbon of liquid silver. Take a moment to dip your fingers into the cool water, feeling its refreshing touch against your skin, cleansing and purifying as it flows past.

Or maybe you stumble upon a hidden glade, bathed in dappled sunlight and alive with the chatter of woodland creatures. Sit down amidst the soft grass and close your eyes, letting yourself be fully present in this moment of quiet serenity. Feel the energy of the earth pulsing beneath you, connecting you to the ancient wisdom of the natural world.

Know that you can return to this mountain meadow whenever you need to find peace and solace amidst the chaos of daily life. Carry the sense of relaxation and tranquility that you've discovered here with you as you journey forward, knowing that you are always connected to the healing power of nature.

When you're ready, slowly begin to bring your awareness back to the present moment, gently opening your eyes and taking a few deep breaths. Take a moment to stretch your limbs and wiggle your fingers and toes, feeling the energy flowing freely through your body once more.

Tropical Rainforest

Welcome to your Tropical Rainforest adventure, a journey into the lush, vibrant world of the rainforest where you can experience the richness of biodiversity and connect with the beauty of nature. Find a comfortable position, either sitting or lying down, and gently close your eyes. Take a deep breath in through your nose, allowing the warm, humid air of the rainforest to fill your lungs, and exhale slowly through your mouth, releasing any tension or stress you may be holding onto.

As you begin your journey, imagine yourself standing at the edge of a dense tropical rainforest, the air heavy with the scent of earth and vegetation, the sounds of chirping birds and buzzing insects filling the air. Take a moment to visualize the towering trees rising high above you, their thick canopy blocking out the sunlight and dappling the forest floor in shade.

Now, let's engage your senses fully as you immerse yourself in the beauty of the rainforest. Close your eyes and listen closely to the sounds of nature—the melodic chirping of birds hidden among the branches, the rhythmic buzz of insects flitting through the air, the gentle rustle of leaves as they sway in the breeze. Let these sounds envelop you, filling you with a sense of wonder and awe at the symphony of life that surrounds you.

As you listen, feel the warmth of the sun on your skin, its rays filtering through the dense canopy above, casting shafts of golden light down to the forest floor. Visualize the vibrant colors of the rainforest—the lush green foliage, the brilliant hues of tropical flowers, the iridescent wings of butterflies flitting through the air. Allow yourself to be captivated by the beauty of your surroundings, finding peace and serenity in the ever-changing landscape.

With each breath you take, feel the moist, humid air of the rainforest filling your lungs, invigorating and refreshing as it cleanses your body and mind. Inhale deeply and breathe in the earthy scent of the forest—the aroma of damp earth and decaying vegetation, the pungent fragrance of tropical flowers and fruits, the sweet scent of nectar carried on the breeze. Let these scents transport you to a place of pure relaxation and bliss.

As you walk deeper into the rainforest, feel the soft, damp earth beneath your feet, the cool, smooth texture of the tree trunks as you run your hands along their rough bark. Reach out and touch the delicate leaves of a fern, the rough surface of a vine, the smooth skin of a tropical fruit hanging from a nearby tree. Let yourself be fully immersed in the tactile sensations of the rainforest, feeling a deep connection to the natural world around you.

Take a moment to pause and gaze up at the towering trees above you, their massive trunks disappearing into the canopy overhead. Marvel at the sheer size and age of these ancient giants, feeling a sense of awe and reverence for the majesty of the rainforest. Listen as the leaves rustle in the breeze, the branches creaking and groaning as they sway in the wind, the occasional crash of a falling fruit or nut echoing through the forest.

As you continue to explore the rainforest, allow yourself to be guided by your curiosity and sense of adventure. Perhaps you come across a sparkling waterfall, its crystal-clear waters cascading down from the heights above, filling the air with the sound of rushing water and the cool mist of its spray. Sit down beside the pool at the base of the waterfall, feeling the refreshing water against your skin, cleansing and rejuvenating as it flows past.

Or maybe you stumble upon a hidden clearing, bathed in sunlight and alive with the vibrant colors and sounds of the rainforest. Take a moment to sit amidst the soft grass and close your eyes, letting yourself be fully present in this moment of quiet serenity. Feel the energy of the earth pulsing beneath you, connecting you to the ancient wisdom of the natural world.

End

or

Extend

Know that you can return to this tropical rainforest whenever you need to find peace and solace amidst the chaos of daily life. Carry the sense of relaxation and tranquility that you've discovered here with you as you journey forward, knowing that you are always connected to the healing power of nature.

When you're ready, slowly begin to bring your awareness back to the present moment, gently opening your eyes and taking a few deep breaths. Take a moment to stretch your limbs and wiggle your fingers and toes, feeling the energy flowing freely through your body once more. ◼

As you stand amidst the lush foliage of the rainforest, take a moment to fully immerse yourself in the vibrant world that surrounds you. Feel the gentle rustle of leaves in the breeze, the cool mist of the waterfall against your skin, the earthy scent of damp soil and decaying vegetation filling your nostrils. With each inhale, feel a sense of peace and connection washing over you, grounding you in the present moment and filling you with a profound sense of gratitude for the beauty of the natural world.

Now, let's deepen your connection to this magical place by engaging your senses even further. With the full power of your imagination, listen closely to the sounds of the rainforest—the rhythmic chirping of crickets, the distant call of a howler monkey echoing through the trees, the gentle patter of raindrops falling on the canopy above. Let these sounds envelop you, transporting you deeper into the heart of the rainforest and filling you with a sense of wonder and awe at the richness of life that surrounds you.

As you listen, feel the warmth of the sun on your skin, its golden rays filtering through the dense foliage overhead and casting intricate patterns of light and shadow on the forest floor. Visualize the vibrant colors of the rainforest—the deep greens of the ferns and mosses, the bright hues of tropical flowers and fruits, the flashing scales of a butterfly gliding through the air.

Allow yourself to be captivated by the beauty of your surroundings, finding peace and serenity in the ever-changing landscape.

With each breath you take, feel the fresh, clean air of the rainforest filling your lungs, invigorating and energizing you from within. Inhale deeply and breathe in the fragrant scents of the forest—the sweet aroma of ripe fruit hanging from the trees, the spicy scent of cinnamon and cloves, the earthy smell of wet leaves and moss. Let these scents transport you to a place of pure relaxation and bliss, where time seems to stand still and the worries of the world melt away.

As you continue to explore the rainforest, allow yourself to be guided by your sense of adventure and curiosity. Perhaps you come across a hidden glade, bathed in sunlight and alive with the vibrant colors and sounds of the forest. Sit down amidst the soft grass and close your eyes, letting yourself be fully present in this moment of quiet serenity. Feel the energy of the earth pulsing beneath you, connecting you to the ancient wisdom of the natural world and filling you with a profound sense of peace and contentment.

Or maybe you stumble upon a rushing river, its crystal-clear waters teeming with life and vitality. Wade into the cool, refreshing water and let it wash over you, cleansing and rejuvenating your body and spirit. Feel the strength and power of the river as it flows past, carrying with it the promise of new beginnings and endless possibilities.

Know that you can return to this tropical rainforest whenever you need to find peace and solace amidst the chaos of daily life. Carry the sense of relaxation and tranquility that you've discovered here with you as you journey forward, knowing that you are always connected to the healing power of nature.

When you're ready, slowly begin to bring your awareness back to the present moment, gently opening your eyes and taking a few deep breaths. Take a moment to stretch your limbs and wiggle your fingers and toes, feeling the energy flowing freely through your body once more. Carry the sense of peace and serenity that you've discovered here with you as you go about your day, knowing that you can always return to the rainforest in your mind whenever you need to find refuge and renewal.

Desert Oasis

Welcome to your Desert Oasis meditation, a journey to a tranquil oasis in the midst of a vast desert landscape where you can experience rejuvenation, renewal, and resilience in the face of adversity. Find a comfortable position, either sitting or lying down, and gently close your eyes. Take a deep breath in through your nose, allowing the warm, dry air of the desert to fill your lungs, and exhale slowly through your mouth, releasing any tension or stress you may be holding onto.

As you begin your journey, imagine yourself standing at the edge of a vast desert, the sun beating down on the golden sands, the heat shimmering in waves across the horizon. Take a moment to visualize the endless expanse of sand stretching out before you, the dunes rising and falling like waves frozen in time.

Now, let's engage your senses fully as you immerse yourself in the beauty of the desert oasis. Close your eyes and listen closely to the sounds of nature—the gentle rustle of palm fronds in the breeze, the distant call of a desert bird echoing across the landscape, the soft murmur of water flowing from the oasis. Let these sounds envelop you, filling you with a sense of peace and tranquility.

As you listen, feel the warmth of the sun on your skin, its rays casting long shadows across the desert floor, the heat radiating from the sand beneath your feet. Visualize the vibrant colors of the oasis—the cool green of palm trees swaying in the breeze, the deep blue of the clear, sparkling water, the rich golden hues of the surrounding sand dunes. Allow yourself to be captivated by the beauty of your surroundings, finding peace and serenity in the simplicity of nature.

With each breath you take, feel the dry, arid air of the desert filling your lungs, invigorating and energizing you from within. Inhale deeply and breathe in the earthy scent of the oasis—the aroma of damp soil and fresh vegetation, the sweet fragrance of blooming flowers, the subtle hint of salt carried on the breeze from the nearby water. Let these scents transport you to a place of pure relaxation and bliss.

As you walk towards the oasis, feel the cool shade of the palm trees enveloping you, their fronds providing shelter from the harsh desert sun. Reach out and touch the rough bark of a palm tree, the smooth texture of its leaves brushing against your fingertips, the refreshing coolness of the water as you dip your hand into the oasis pool. Let yourself be fully immersed in the tactile sensations of the oasis, feeling a deep connection to the natural world around you.

Take a moment to pause and gaze out at the tranquil waters of the oasis, its surface shimmering in the sunlight like a mirror reflecting the beauty of the surrounding landscape. Marvel at the abundance of life that thrives in this harsh desert environment, from the lush greenery of the palm trees to the delicate blooms of desert flowers that line the water's edge. Listen as the breeze rustles through the palm fronds, the gentle lapping of water against the shore, the distant hum of insects buzzing in the air.

As you sit beside the oasis, allow yourself to be lulled into a state of deep relaxation by the soothing sounds and sights of nature. Feel a sense of peace and contentment wash over you, filling you with a profound sense of gratitude for the opportunity to experience such beauty and tranquility amidst the harshness of the desert.

End ⟶ Know that you can return to this desert oasis whenever you need to find refuge and renewal in the face of adversity. Carry the sense of relaxation and tranquility that you've discovered here with you as you journey forward, knowing that you are always connected to the healing power of nature.

or

Extend

When you're ready, slowly begin to bring your awareness back to the present moment, gently opening your eyes and taking a few deep breaths. Take a moment to stretch your limbs and wiggle your fingers and toes, feeling the energy flowing freely through your body once more. ∎

As you sit beside the oasis, allow yourself to sink deeper into a state of profound relaxation and tranquility. Feel the cool, refreshing water lapping gently against your skin, soothing and revitalizing you from within. With each breath you take, feel a sense of renewal and rejuvenation washing over you, cleansing your body and mind of any lingering tension or stress.

Now, let's deepen your connection to this sacred place of refuge and renewal by engaging your senses even further. Close your eyes once more, using the full power of your imagination and listen closely to the sounds of the oasis—the soft rustle of palm fronds in the breeze, the gentle splashing of water as it cascades over rocks, the melodious chirping of birds perched in the nearby trees. Let these sounds envelop you, transporting you deeper into a state of inner peace and tranquility.

As you listen, feel the warmth of the sun on your skin, its rays filtering through the palm fronds overhead, casting dancing patterns of light and shadow on the ground below. Visualize the vibrant colors of the oasis—the deep emerald green of the palm trees, the shimmering turquoise of the water, the golden hues of the sand dunes stretching out to the horizon. Allow yourself to be captivated by the beauty of your surroundings, finding solace and serenity in the timeless tranquility of the desert oasis.

With each breath you take, feel the clean, crisp air of the desert filling your lungs, invigorating and energizing you from within. Inhale deeply and breathe in the fragrant scents of the oasis—the earthy aroma of wet soil and vegetation, the sweet perfume of blooming flowers, the subtle hint of minerals carried on the breeze from the underground springs. Let these scents envelop you, transporting you to a place of pure relaxation and bliss.

As you continue to explore the oasis, allow yourself to be guided by your intuition and sense of wonder. Perhaps you come across a hidden alcove, tucked away behind a veil of cascading waterfalls, where the air is cool and misty, and the sunlight filters through the canopy in shifting patterns of light and shadow. Sit down amidst the moss-covered rocks and close your eyes, letting yourself be fully present in this moment of quiet serenity. Feel the energy of the earth pulsing beneath you, connecting you to the ancient wisdom of the natural world and filling you with a sense of peace and contentment.

Or maybe you stumble upon a tranquil lagoon among the dunes, its crystal-clear waters from underground aquifers teeming with life and vitality. Wade into the cool, refreshing water and let it envelop you, cleansing and rejuvenating your body and spirit. Feel the gentle current as it flows past, carrying with it the promise of new beginnings and endless possibilities.

Know that you can return to this desert oasis whenever you need to find refuge and renewal in the face of adversity. Carry the sense of relaxation and tranquility that you've discovered here with you as you journey forward, knowing that you are always connected to the healing power of nature.

    When you're ready, slowly begin to bring your awareness back to the present moment, gently opening your eyes and taking a few deep breaths. Take a moment to stretch your limbs and wiggle your fingers and toes, feeling the energy flowing freely through your body once more. Carry the sense of peace and serenity that you've discovered here with you as you go about your day, knowing that you can always return to the oasis in your mind whenever you need to find refuge and renewal.

Enchanted Forest

Welcome to your Enchanted Forest adventure, a journey into a mystical realm filled with ancient trees, winding pathways, and hidden glades where magic and wonder abound. Find a comfortable position, either sitting or lying down, and gently close your eyes. Take a deep breath in through your nose, allowing the fresh, earthy scent of the forest to fill your lungs, and exhale slowly through your mouth, releasing any tension or stress you may be holding onto.

As you begin your journey, imagine yourself standing at the edge of a dense forest, the sunlight filtering through the canopy overhead, casting intricate patterns of light and shadow on the forest floor. Take a moment to visualize the towering trees rising high above you, their branches reaching towards the sky like ancient sentinels guarding the secrets of the forest.

Now, let's engage your senses fully as you immerse yourself in the beauty of the enchanted forest. Close your eyes and listen closely to the sounds of nature—the gentle rustle of leaves in the breeze, the distant call of birdsong echoing through the trees, the soft chirping of crickets hidden in the underbrush. Let these sounds envelop you, filling you with a sense of peace and tranquility.

As you listen, feel the cool, damp earth beneath your feet, the soft moss and fallen leaves cushioning your steps as you walk deeper into the forest. Visualize the vibrant colors of the forest—the deep greens of the ferns and ivy, the rich browns of the tree trunks, the delicate hues of wildflowers blooming along the forest floor. Allow yourself to be captivated by the beauty of your surroundings, feeling a sense of wonder and awe at the magic that lies hidden within the forest.

With each breath you take, feel the clean, crisp air of the forest filling your lungs, invigorating and energizing you from within. Inhale deeply and breathe in the earthy scent of the forest—the aroma of damp soil and decaying vegetation, the sweet fragrance of wildflowers and herbs, the subtle hint of pine carried on the breeze. Let these scents transport you to a place of pure relaxation and bliss.

As you walk along the winding pathways of the forest, allow yourself to be guided by your curiosity and sense of wonder. Perhaps you come across a hidden glade, bathed in dappled sunlight and alive with the vibrant colors and sounds of nature. Sit down amidst the soft grass and close your eyes, letting yourself be fully present in this moment of quiet serenity. Feel the energy of the earth pulsing beneath you, connecting you to the ancient wisdom of the natural world and filling you with a sense of peace and contentment.

Or maybe you stumble upon a secret grove, where the trees are twisted and gnarled, their branches forming intricate patterns against the sky. Step into the grove and feel the air grow thick with magic and mystery, as if you've entered a realm beyond the ordinary world. Listen as the leaves whisper secrets in the breeze, the branches creak and groan as if alive, the air tingling with the energy of unseen forces.

End
or
Extend

Know that you can return to this enchanted forest whenever you need to find solace and inspiration in the midst of the chaos of daily life. Carry the sense of wonder and magic that you've discovered here with you as you journey forward, knowing that you are always connected to the mystical realms of the natural world.

When you're ready, slowly begin to bring your awareness back to the present moment, gently opening your eyes and taking a few deep breaths. Take a moment to stretch your limbs and wiggle your fingers and toes, feeling the energy flowing freely through your body once more. ■

As you sit in the heart of the enchanted forest, allow yourself to sink deeper into a state of profound peace and tranquility. Feel the gentle rustle of leaves in the breeze, the soft whisper of branches overhead, the cool touch of moss and ferns beneath your fingertips. With each breath you take, feel a sense of connection and belonging wash over you, as if you've come home to a place of deep-rooted magic and wonder.

Now, let's deepen your connection to this mystical realm by engaging your senses even further. Listen closely to the sounds of the forest—the rhythmic chirping of crickets, the soothing babble of a nearby stream, the distant call of a nocturnal creature awakening as night falls. Let these sounds envelop you, transporting you deeper into a state of inner peace and harmony.

As you listen, feel the cool, refreshing air of the forest filling your lungs, invigorating and revitalizing you from within. Inhale deeply and breathe in the earthy scent of the forest—the aroma of damp soil and fallen leaves, the sweet fragrance of wildflowers blooming in the moonlight, the subtle hint of woodsmoke carried on the breeze from a distant campfire. Let these scents transport you to a place of pure relaxation and bliss.

As you continue to explore the enchanted forest, allow yourself to be guided by your intuition and sense of wonder. Perhaps you come across a hidden clearing, bathed in the soft glow of moonlight filtering through the trees. Sit down amidst the soft grass and close your eyes, letting yourself be fully present in this moment of quiet serenity. Feel the energy of the earth pulsing beneath you, connecting you to the ancient wisdom of the natural world and filling you with a sense of peace and contentment.

Or maybe you stumble upon a secret garden, where the air is heavy with the scent of exotic blooms and the ground is carpeted with lush greenery. Step into the garden and feel the air come alive with magic and possibility, as if you've entered a realm where dreams and reality intertwine. Listen as the flowers whisper secrets in the night breeze, the stars overhead twinkling like diamonds in the sky, the air alive with the gentle hum of unseen creatures.

Know that you can return to this enchanted forest whenever you need to find solace and inspiration in the midst of the chaos of daily life. Carry the sense of wonder and magic that you've discovered here with you as you journey forward, knowing that you are always connected to the mystical realms of the natural world.

When you're ready, slowly begin to bring your awareness back to the present moment, gently opening your eyes and taking a few deep breaths. Take a moment to stretch your limbs and wiggle your fingers and toes, feeling the energy flowing freely through your body once more. Carry the sense of peace and serenity that you've discovered here with you as you go about your day, knowing that you can always return to the enchanted forest in your mind whenever you need to find refuge and renewal.

Mountain Lake

Welcome to your Mountain Lake meditation, a journey to a tranquil oasis nestled among towering mountains where you can experience serenity, reflection, and connection to the beauty of nature. Find a comfortable position, either sitting or lying down, and gently close your eyes. Take a deep breath in through your nose, allowing the crisp, mountain air to fill your lungs, and exhale slowly through your mouth, releasing any tension or stress you may be holding onto.

As you begin your journey, imagine yourself standing at the edge of a pristine lake, its mirror-like surface reflecting the towering peaks that surround it, the sunlight sparkling on the water like diamonds. Take a moment to visualize the rugged beauty of the mountains, their snow-capped summits reaching towards the sky, their rocky slopes covered in lush greenery and colorful wildflowers.

Now, let's engage your senses fully as you immerse yourself in the tranquility of the mountain lake. With closed eyes, listen closely to the sounds of nature—the gentle lapping of water against the shore, the distant cry of an eagle soaring overhead, the soft rustle of leaves in the breeze. Let these sounds envelop you, filling you with a sense of peace and tranquility.

As you listen, feel the cool, clear water of the lake lapping gently against your feet, the smooth pebbles and soft sand beneath your toes. Visualize the vibrant colors of the lake—the deep blue of the water, the emerald green of the surrounding forests, the brilliant white of the snow-capped peaks reflected in its surface. Allow yourself to be captivated by the beauty of your surroundings, feeling a sense of awe and wonder at the majesty of nature.

With each breath you take, feel the clean, crisp air of the mountains filling your lungs, invigorating and energizing you from within. Inhale deeply and breathe in the fresh, pine-scented air—the aroma of evergreen trees, the earthy scent of damp soil and fallen leaves, the subtle hint of wildflowers carried on the breeze. Let these scents transport you to a place of pure relaxation and bliss.

As you gaze out across the tranquil expanse of the lake, allow yourself to be drawn into a state of deep reflection and introspection. Take a moment to contemplate the beauty and wonder of the natural world, the interconnectedness of all living things, the timeless rhythms of the earth. Feel a sense of gratitude and reverence welling up within you, as you realize your own small place in the vast tapestry of life.

With each passing moment, feel a sense of peace and serenity wash over you, as if the very essence of the mountain lake is seeping into your soul. Allow yourself to be fully present in this moment, letting go of any worries or distractions, and simply basking in the beauty of the world around you.

Now, let's deepen your connection to this sacred place of reflection and renewal by engaging your senses even further. Listen hard to all the sounds of the lake—

the rhythmic lapping of waves against the shore, the melodic chirping of birds hidden in the trees, the distant rumble of a waterfall cascading down the mountainside. Let these sounds envelop you, transporting you deeper into a state of inner peace and harmony.

As you listen, feel the cool, refreshing water of the lake enveloping you, cleansing and rejuvenating your body and spirit. Inhale deeply and breathe in the crisp, clean air of the mountains, feeling it fill your lungs and invigorate your senses. With each breath you take, feel a sense of renewal and revitalization wash over you, as if the very essence of the mountain lake is infusing you with its healing energy.

As you continue to explore the mountain lake, allow yourself to be guided by your intuition and sense of wonder. Perhaps you come across a hidden cove, where the water is calm and still, and the air is alive with the gentle hum of dragonflies and butterflies flitting about. Sit down beside the lake and close your eyes, letting yourself be fully present in this moment of quiet serenity. Feel the energy of the earth pulsing beneath you, connecting you to the ancient wisdom of the natural world and filling you with a sense of peace and contentment.

Or maybe you stumble upon a secluded beach, where the sand is soft and warm beneath your feet, and the water is crystal clear and inviting. Wade into the lake and let its cool embrace envelop you, cleansing and purifying your body and spirit. Feel the weight of the world lift from your shoulders as you surrender to the healing power of the mountain lake, knowing that you are safe and supported in this sacred space.

End

or

Extend

⟶ Know that you can return to this mountain lake whenever you need to find solace and renewal in the midst of the chaos of daily life. Carry the sense of peace and serenity that you've discovered here with you as you journey forward, knowing that you are always connected to the healing power of nature.

> When you're ready, slowly begin to bring your awareness back to the present moment, gently opening your eyes and taking a few deep breaths. Take a moment to stretch your limbs and wiggle your fingers and toes, feeling the energy flowing freely through your body once more. ∎

As you sit beside the mountain lake, allow yourself to sink deeper into a state of profound peace and tranquility. Feel the gentle rhythm of your breath as it rises and falls, mirroring the ebb and flow of the water before you. With each breath you take, feel a sense of connection and harmony with the natural world around you, as if you are one with the mountains, the lake, and the sky.

Now, let's deepen your connection to this sacred place of reflection and renewal by engaging your senses even further. Listen closely to the sounds of the mountain lake—the soothing symphony of water lapping against the shore, the melodious trill of songbirds perched in the nearby trees, the distant echo of a waterfall cascading down the mountainside. Let these sounds envelop you, transporting you deeper into a state of inner peace and tranquility.

As you listen, feel the cool, refreshing water of the lake enveloping you, cleansing and rejuvenating your body and spirit. Inhale deeply and breathe in the crisp, clean air of the mountains, feeling it fill your lungs and invigorate your senses. With each breath you take, feel a sense of renewal and revitalization wash over you, as if the very essence of the mountain lake is infusing you with its healing energy.

Now, let's explore the depths of the mountain lake together. Visualize yourself diving beneath the surface of the water, feeling the cool embrace of the lake as you descend deeper and deeper into its depths. Allow yourself to be enveloped by the silence and stillness of the underwater world, as if you are suspended in time and space, weightless and free.

As you explore the underwater landscape, marvel at the vibrant colors and diverse array of life that thrives beneath the surface of the lake. Watch as schools of fish dart gracefully through the water, their scales shimmering in the dappled sunlight filtering down from above. Listen as the gentle hum of underwater currents carries you along, the rhythmic beat of your own heart echoing in your ears.

As you continue to explore the depths of the mountain lake, allow yourself to be captivated by the beauty and wonder of the underwater world. Glide past towering rock formations and hidden caves, their walls adorned with delicate corals and shimmering crystals. Marvel at the intricate dance of light and shadow that plays across the sandy bottom, as shafts of sunlight filter down from the surface above.

Take a moment to pause and gaze out at the vast expanse of the lake stretching out before you, its surface shimmering in the sunlight like a mirror reflecting the beauty of the surrounding landscape. Feel a sense of peace and serenity wash over you as you realize the interconnectedness of all living things, the harmony and balance that exists within the natural world.

Know that you can return to this mountain lake whenever you need to find solace and renewal in the midst of the chaos of daily life. Carry the sense of peace and serenity that you've discovered here with you as you journey forward, knowing that you are always connected to the healing power of nature.

When you're ready, slowly begin to bring your awareness back to the present moment, gently opening your eyes and taking a few deep breaths. Take a moment to stretch your limbs and wiggle your fingers and toes, feeling the energy flowing freely through your body once more. Carry the sense of peace and serenity that you've discovered here with you as you go about your day, knowing that you can always return to the mountain lake in your mind whenever you need to find refuge and renewal.

Canyon Serenity

Welcome to your Canyon Serenity meditation, a journey into the heart of a majestic canyon where you can experience the awe-inspiring beauty and tranquility of nature. Find a comfortable position, either sitting or lying down, and gently close your eyes. Take a deep breath in through your nose, allowing the crisp, clean air to fill your lungs, and exhale slowly through your mouth, releasing any tension or stress you may be holding onto.

As you begin your journey, imagine yourself standing at the edge of a vast canyon, surrounded by towering cliffs that rise up on either side of you. Visualize the rugged landscape stretching out before you, the rocky terrain carved by centuries of wind and water, and the gentle river winding its way through the canyon floor. Take a moment to marvel at the sheer scale and grandeur of the landscape, feeling a sense of awe and wonder wash over you.

Now, let's engage your senses fully as you immerse yourself in the serenity of the canyon. Close your eyes and listen closely to the sounds of nature—the soothing rush of water as it cascades over rocks, the soft rustle of leaves in the breeze, the distant call of birds echoing off the canyon walls. Let these sounds envelop you, transporting you deeper into a state of inner peace and tranquility.

As you listen, feel the rough texture of the canyon walls beneath your fingertips, the cool, smooth surface of the rocks worn smooth by time and weather. Visualize the interplay of light and shadow on the canyon walls—the warm glow of sunlight filtering through the cracks and crevices, the deep shadows cast by the towering cliffs overhead. Allow yourself to be captivated by the ever-changing patterns and textures of the landscape, feeling a sense of connection and belonging to the natural world.

With each breath you take, feel the clean, crisp air of the canyon filling your lungs, invigorating and energizing you from within. Inhale deeply and breathe in the earthy scent of the rocks and soil—the aroma of sun-warmed stone, the subtle hint of sagebrush carried on the breeze. Let these scents transport you to a place of pure relaxation and bliss.

As you explore the canyon, allow yourself to be guided by your intuition and sense of wonder. Perhaps you come across a hidden alcove, where a small waterfall tumbles down from above, forming a crystal-clear pool at its base. Sit down beside the pool and close your eyes, letting yourself be fully present in this moment of quiet serenity. Feel the energy of the earth pulsing beneath you, connecting you to the ancient wisdom of the natural world and filling you with a sense of peace and contentment.

Or maybe you stumble upon a secluded overlook, where you can watch the sun set behind the distant peaks, casting the canyon in a warm, golden light. Sit down on a nearby rock and close your eyes, letting yourself be enveloped by the beauty and stillness of the moment. Listen as the sounds of nature fade into the background, replaced by the gentle hum of your own breath and the rhythmic beating of your heart.

End ⟶ Know that you can return to this canyon whenever you need to find solace and renewal in the midst of the chaos of daily life. Carry the sense of peace and serenity that you've discovered here with you as you journey forward, knowing that you are always connected to the healing power of nature.

or

Extend

When you're ready, slowly begin to bring your awareness back to the present moment, gently opening your eyes and taking a few deep breaths. Take a moment to stretch your limbs and wiggle your fingers and toes, feeling the energy flowing freely through your body once more. ■

▼ As you sit beside the canyon, allow yourself to sink deeper into a state of profound peace and tranquility. Feel the warmth of the sun on your skin, the gentle breeze rustling through your hair, and the solid earth beneath you, grounding and supporting you in this sacred space. With each breath you take, feel a sense of connection and harmony with the natural world around you, as if you are one with the canyon itself.

Now, let's deepen your connection to this sacred place of reflection and renewal by engaging your senses even further. With closed eyes, listen closely to all the sounds of the canyon—the soothing rush of water as it cascades over rocks, the gentle rustle of leaves in the breeze, the distant cry of a hawk soaring high above. Let these sounds envelop you, transporting you deeper into a state of inner peace and tranquility.

As you listen, feel the cool, clear water of the river lapping gently against the shore, the smooth stones and pebbles beneath your feet, worn smooth by centuries of erosion. Visualize the vibrant colors of the canyon—the rich reds, oranges, and yellows of the rock formations, the deep greens of the trees and shrubs that cling to the canyon walls. Allow yourself to be captivated by the beauty and diversity of life that thrives in this rugged landscape, feeling a sense of reverence and respect for the natural world.

With each breath you take, feel the clean, crisp air of the canyon filling your lungs, invigorating and energizing you from within. Inhale deeply and breathe in the earthy scent of the rocks and soil—the aroma of sun-warmed stone, the subtle hint of sagebrush carried on the breeze. Let these scents transport you to a place of pure relaxation and bliss.

As you explore the canyon, allow yourself to be guided by your intuition and sense of wonder. Perhaps you come across a hidden cave, where the air is cool and damp, and the walls are adorned with ancient petroglyphs and pictographs left behind by the canyon's earliest inhabitants. Step inside the cave and close your eyes, letting yourself be fully present in this moment of quiet serenity. Feel the energy of the earth pulsing beneath you, connecting you to the ancient wisdom of the natural world and filling you with a sense of peace and contentment.

Or maybe you stumble upon a secluded spot along the riverbank, where the water is calm and still, and the only sounds are the gentle rustle of leaves and the occasional splash of a fish breaking the surface. Sit down beside the river and close your eyes, letting yourself be enveloped by the beauty and stillness of the moment. Listen as the sounds of nature fade into the background, replaced by the gentle hum of your own breath and the rhythmic beating of your heart.

Know that you can return to this canyon whenever you need to find solace and renewal in the midst of the chaos of daily life. Carry the sense of peace and serenity that you've discovered here with you as you journey forward, knowing that you are always connected to the healing power of nature.

When you're ready, slowly begin to bring your awareness back to the present moment, gently opening your eyes and taking a few deep breaths. Take a moment to stretch your limbs and wiggle your fingers and toes, feeling the energy flowing freely through your body once more.

Mystical Cavern

Welcome to your Mystical Cavern meditation, a journey into the depths of a hidden world where magic and mystery await. Find a comfortable position, either sitting or lying down, and gently close your eyes. Take a deep breath in through your nose, allowing the cool, damp air of the cavern to fill your lungs, and exhale slowly through your mouth, releasing any tension or stress you may be holding onto.

As you begin your journey, imagine yourself standing at the entrance of a hidden cavern, its ancient stone walls beckoning you into the depths. Visualize the towering stalactites that hang like icicles from the ceiling, their shimmering surfaces reflecting the soft glow of bioluminescent fungi that carpet the cavern floor. Take a moment to marvel at the beauty and wonder of this hidden world, feeling a sense of anticipation and excitement building within you.

Now, let's engage your senses fully as you immerse yourself in the mystery of the cavern. Close your eyes and listen closely to the sounds of the underground—the faint drip of water echoing off the walls, the soft rustle of bats' wings as they flit overhead, the distant rumble of underground rivers carving their way through the earth. Let these sounds envelop you, transporting you deeper into a state of inner peace and tranquility.

As you listen, feel the cool, damp air of the cavern on your skin, the moisture clinging to your clothes and hair, the soft earth beneath your feet. Visualize the intricate patterns and textures of the cavern walls—the rough, uneven surface of the stone, the intricate patterns of mineral deposits that sparkle in the faint light. Allow yourself to be captivated by the ancient beauty of this hidden world, feeling a sense of wonder and reverence for the mysteries it holds.

With each breath you take, feel the cool, crisp air of the cavern filling your lungs, invigorating and energizing you from within. Inhale deeply and breathe in the earthy scent of the rock and soil—the aroma of damp stone, the subtle hint of moss and lichen growing in the shadows. Let these scents transport you to a place of pure relaxation and bliss.

As you explore the cavern, allow yourself to be guided by your intuition and sense of wonder. Perhaps you come across a crystal-clear pool, its surface rippling gently in the faint light, reflecting the shimmering glow of bioluminescent fungi that carpet the cavern floor. Dip your hand into the cool, clear water and feel its refreshing touch on your skin, cleansing and rejuvenating you from within. Close your eyes and let yourself be fully present in this moment of quiet serenity, feeling a sense of connection and harmony with the natural world around you.

Or maybe you stumble upon a hidden chamber, where the walls are adorned with intricate carvings and glyphs, telling the stories of the ancient people who once inhabited this sacred space. Sit down beside the chamber and close your eyes, letting yourself be enveloped by the beauty and mystery of the moment.

Listen as the sounds of the cavern fade into the background, replaced by the gentle hum of your own breath and the rhythmic beating of your heart.

End ⟶ Know that you can return to this mystical cavern whenever you need to find solace and renewal in the midst of the chaos of daily life. Carry the sense of peace and serenity that you've discovered here with you as you journey forward, knowing that you are always connected to the healing power of nature.

or

Extend

When you're ready, slowly begin to bring your awareness back to the present moment, gently opening your eyes and taking a few deep breaths. Take a moment to stretch your limbs and wiggle your fingers and toes, feeling the energy flowing freely through your body once more. ∎

As you sit in the heart of the mystical cavern, allow yourself to sink deeper into a state of profound peace and tranquility. Feel the cool, damp air surrounding you, wrapping you in its embrace like a soft, comforting blanket. With each breath you take, feel a sense of calm and relaxation wash over you, as if all your worries and cares are melting away into the darkness of the cavern.

Now, let's deepen your connection to this sacred space by engaging your senses even further. Listen closely to the sounds of the cavern—the gravel crunching underfoot echoing off the walls, the distant clicks and screeches of faraway bats, the distant murmur of underground streams flowing far below. Let these sounds envelop you, transporting you deeper into a state of inner peace and tranquility.

As you listen, feel the smooth, cool stone of the cavern walls beneath your fingertips, the rough texture of the rock worn smooth by centuries of erosion. Visualize the amazing formations of the stalactites and stalagmites—their otherworldly shapes and sizes creating a mesmerizing display of natural beauty. Allow yourself to be captivated by the ancient magic of the cavern, feeling a sense of wonder and reverence for the mysteries it holds.

With each breath you take, feel the cool, crisp air of the cavern filling your lungs, invigorating and energizing you from within. Inhale deeply and breathe in the earthy scent of the rock and soil—the aroma of damp stone, the subtle hint of minerals and ancient earth. Let these scents transport you to a place of pure relaxation and bliss.

As you explore the cavern, allow yourself to be guided by your intuition and sense of curiosity. Perhaps you come across a hidden passage, leading deeper into the heart of the cavern, where the darkness seems to thicken and the air grows colder. Step forward with courage and curiosity, trusting in the wisdom of your inner guide to lead you safely through the darkness.

Or maybe you stumble upon a chamber filled with bioluminescent glowworms, their soft light illuminating the darkness with an ethereal glow. Sit down beside the dazzling light and widen your eyes, letting yourself be fully present in this moment of quiet serenity. Feel the energy of the earth pulsing beneath you, connecting you to the ancient wisdom of the natural world and filling you with a sense of peace and contentment.

Know that you can return to this mystical cavern whenever you need to find solace and renewal in the midst of the chaos of daily life. Carry the sense of peace and serenity that you've discovered here with you as you journey forward, knowing that you are always connected to the healing power of nature.

When you're ready, slowly begin to bring your awareness back to the present moment, gently opening your eyes and taking a few deep breaths. Take a moment to stretch your limbs and wiggle your fingers and toes, feeling the energy flowing freely through your body once more.

Arctic Tundra

Welcome to your Arctic Tundra meditation, a journey into the vast, frozen wilderness of the north where the beauty and majesty of the tundra await. Find a comfortable position, either sitting or lying down, and gently close your eyes. Take a deep breath in through your nose, allowing the crisp, clean air of the Arctic to fill your lungs, and exhale slowly through your mouth, releasing any tension or stress you may be holding onto.

As you begin your journey, imagine yourself standing on the edge of the Arctic tundra, surrounded by a landscape of snow and ice that stretches out as far as the eye can see. Visualize the hardy shrubs and lichen-covered rocks that dot the frozen landscape, their vibrant colors standing out against the stark white backdrop of snow. Take a moment to marvel at the sheer vastness and beauty of the tundra, feeling a sense of awe and wonder wash over you.

Now, let's engage your senses fully as you immerse yourself in the beauty of the Arctic. Close your eyes and listen closely to the sounds of the tundra—the soft crunch of snow beneath your feet, the distant call of a bird soaring overhead, the gentle rustle of the wind as it sweeps across the frozen landscape. Let these sounds envelop you, transporting you deeper into a state of inner peace and tranquility.

As you listen, feel the cold, crisp air of the tundra on your skin, the icy chill biting at your cheeks and nose. Visualize the endless expanse of snow and ice stretching out before you, the shimmering surface of frozen lakes and rivers reflecting the pale light of the Arctic sun. Allow yourself to be captivated by the stark beauty of this frozen wilderness, feeling a sense of connection and belonging to the natural world.

With each breath you take, feel the clean, pure air of the tundra filling your lungs, invigorating and energizing you from within. Inhale deeply and breathe in the scent of the Arctic—the crisp aroma of snow and ice, the subtle hint of pine carried on the breeze. Let these scents transport you to a place of pure relaxation and bliss.

As you explore the tundra, allow yourself to be guided by your intuition and sense of wonder. Perhaps you come across a herd of caribou, their thick fur coats keeping them warm in the cold Arctic air. Watch as they graze on the sparse vegetation that grows beneath the snow, their graceful movements a testament to the resilience and strength of life in the north.

Or maybe you stumble upon a frozen waterfall, its crystalline surface shimmering in the light of the Arctic sun. Stand before the waterfall and close your eyes, letting yourself be fully present in this moment of quiet serenity. Listen as the sounds of the tundra fade into the background, replaced by the gentle hum of your own breath and the rhythmic beating of your heart.

End ⟶ Know that you can return to this Arctic tundra whenever you need to find solace and renewal in the midst of the

or

Extend
↓

chaos of daily life. Carry the sense of peace and serenity that you've discovered here with you as you journey forward, knowing that you are always connected to the healing power of nature.

When you're ready, slowly begin to bring your awareness back to the present moment, gently opening your eyes and taking a few deep breaths. Take a moment to stretch your limbs and wiggle your fingers and toes, feeling the energy flowing freely through your body once more. ■

As you stand amidst the vast expanse of the Arctic tundra, allow yourself to sink deeper into a state of profound peace and tranquility. Feel the icy chill of the air surrounding you, the cold seeping into your bones and awakening your senses. With each breath you take, feel a sense of calm and stillness wash over you, as if you are becoming one with the frozen landscape.

Now, let's deepen your connection to this remote wilderness by engaging your senses even further. Listen closely to all the sounds of the tundra—the gentle whisper of the wind as it sweeps across the frozen landscape, the distant howl of a wolf echoing through the icy silence, the crackle of ice as it shifts and groans beneath your feet. Let these sounds envelop you, transporting you deeper into a state of inner peace and tranquility.

As you listen, feel the cold, crisp air of the tundra on your skin, the frosty breeze tingling against your cheeks and nose. Visualize the endless expanse of snow and ice stretching out before you, the vastness of the landscape stretching to the horizon and beyond. Allow yourself to be captivated by the stark beauty of this frozen wilderness, feeling a sense of reverence and awe for the power and majesty of nature.

With each new breath, feel the sharp air of the tundra filling your lungs, awakening you from within. Inhale deeply and breathe in the scent of the Arctic—the crisp aroma of snow and ice, the faint hint of moss and lichen carried on the breeze. Let these scents calm you and connect you to your true nature of being.

As you explore the tundra, allow yourself to be guided by your intuition and sense of adventure. Perhaps you come across a hidden ice cave, its entrance partially obscured by snow and ice. Step inside the cave and close your eyes, letting yourself be fully present in this moment of quiet serenity. Listen as the sounds of the tundra fade into the background, replaced by the soft echo of your own breath and the rhythmic drip of melting ice.

Or maybe you stumble upon a frozen lake, its surface shimmering in the light of the Arctic sun. Sit down beside the lake and close your eyes, letting yourself be enveloped by the beauty and stillness of the moment. Listen as the sounds of nature fade into the background, replaced by the gentle hum of your own breath and the rhythmic beating of your heart.

Know that you can return to this Arctic tundra whenever you need to find solace and renewal in the midst of the chaos of daily life. Carry the sense of peace and serenity that you've discovered here with you as you journey forward, knowing that you are always connected to the healing power of nature.

When you're ready, slowly begin to bring your awareness back to the present moment, gently opening your eyes and taking a few deep breaths. Take a moment to stretch your limbs and wiggle your fingers and toes, feeling the energy flowing freely through your body once more.

Sunset Overlook

Welcome to your Sunset Overlook meditation, a journey to a breathtaking vantage point where you can witness the beauty of nature's grand finale—the setting sun. Find a comfortable position, either sitting or lying down, and gently close your eyes. Take a deep breath in through your nose, allowing the anticipation of the sunset to fill your lungs, and exhale slowly through your mouth, releasing any tension or stress you may be holding onto.

As you begin your journey, imagine yourself standing on the edge of a cliff, overlooking a vast expanse of land and sky. Visualize the warm hues of orange, pink, and gold painting the sky as the sun barely dips below the horizon, casting a soft glow over the landscape. Take a moment to marvel at the sheer beauty and majesty of the sunset, feeling a sense of awe and wonder wash over you.

Now, let's engage your senses fully as you immerse yourself in the beauty of the sunset. Close your eyes and listen closely to the sounds of nature—the gentle rustle of leaves in the breeze, the distant call of birds returning to their nests, the soothing murmur of water flowing nearby. Let these sounds envelop you, transporting you deeper into a state of inner peace and tranquility.

As you listen, feel the warmth of the fading sunlight on your skin, the gentle caress of the breeze ruffling your hair. Visualize the vibrant colors of the sunset—the fiery oranges, the rosy pinks, the golden yellows—stretching across the sky like a canvas painted by the hand of the divine. Allow yourself to be captivated by the beauty and serenity of this moment, feeling a sense of connection and harmony with the natural world.

With each breath you take, feel the cool, refreshing air of the evening filling your lungs, invigorating and energizing you from within. Inhale deeply and breathe in the scent of the earth—the aroma of grass and flowers, the subtle hint of pine carried on the breeze. Let these scents transport you to a place of pure relaxation and bliss.

As you watch the sunset unfold before you, allow yourself to be fully present in this moment of quiet serenity. Notice how the colors of the sky shift and change with each passing moment, creating a symphony of light and color that dances across the horizon. Feel a sense of peace and contentment wash over you as you witness the beauty of the sunset, knowing that you are exactly where you need to be in this moment.

End ⟶ Know that you can return to this Sunset Overlook whenever you need to find solace and renewal in the midst of the chaos of daily life. Carry the sense of peace and serenity that you've discovered here with you as you journey forward, knowing that you are always connected to the beauty and wonder of the natural world.

or

Extend

> When you're ready, slowly begin to bring your awareness back to the present moment, gently opening your eyes and taking a few deep breaths. Take a moment to stretch your limbs and wiggle your fingers and toes, feeling the energy flowing freely through your body once more. ∎

As you continue to watch the sunset unfold before you, allow yourself to sink deeper into a state of profound peace and tranquility. Feel the warmth of the fading sunlight on your skin, the soft glow of the sky enveloping you like a warm embrace. With each breath you take, feel a sense of calm and serenity wash over you, as if all your worries and cares are melting away with the setting sun.

Now, let's deepen your connection to this magical moment by engaging your senses even further. Listen hard for all the sounds of the evening—the gentle hum of insects in the air, the distant cooing of birds settling into their nests, the rhythmic lapping of waves against the shore below. Let these sounds envelop you, transporting you deeper into a state of inner peace and tranquility.

As you listen, feel the cool, refreshing air of the evening on your skin, the soft caress of the breeze brushing against your cheeks and hair. Visualize the changing colors of the sky—the rich hues of purple and blue blending seamlessly with the fiery oranges and pinks of the sunset. Allow yourself to be captivated by the beauty and splendor of this moment, feeling a sense of gratitude and wonder for the gift of life and nature.

With each breath you take, feel the energy of the earth coursing through your veins, invigorating and energizing you from within. Inhale deeply and breathe in the scent of the evening—the aroma of flowers in bloom, the earthy fragrance of the soil beneath your feet. Let these scents transport you to a place of pure relaxation and bliss.

As you watch the last rays of sunlight disappear below the horizon, allow yourself to be fully present in this moment of quiet serenity. Notice how the world around you seems to slow down and soften, as if time itself has paused to savor the beauty of the sunset. Feel a sense of peace and contentment wash over you as you bask in the afterglow of the evening, knowing that you are exactly where you need to be in this moment.

Know that you can return to this Sunset Overlook whenever you need to find solace and renewal in the midst of the chaos of daily life. Carry the sense of peace and serenity that you've discovered here with you as you journey forward, knowing that you are always connected to the beauty and wonder of the natural world.

When you're ready, slowly begin to bring your awareness back to the present moment, gently opening your eyes and taking a few deep breaths. Take a moment to stretch your limbs and wiggle your fingers and toes, feeling the energy flowing freely through your body once more.

Celestial Observatory

Welcome to your Celestial Observatory meditation, a journey to a secluded mountaintop observatory where you can marvel at the wonders of the cosmos. Find a comfortable position, either sitting or lying down, and gently close your eyes. Take a deep breath in through your nose, allowing the anticipation of stargazing to fill your lungs, and exhale slowly through your mouth, releasing any tension or stress you may be holding onto.

As you begin your journey, imagine yourself standing outside a secluded observatory nestled high in the mountains. Visualize the crisp, clear night sky stretching out before you, the twinkling stars overhead casting a soft glow over the landscape. Take a moment to appreciate the beauty and majesty of the cosmos, feeling a sense of awe and wonder wash over you.

Now, let's engage your senses fully as you immerse yourself in the beauty of the night sky. Close your eyes and listen closely to the sounds of the night—the soft whisper of the wind in the trees, the distant hoot of an owl echoing through the darkness, the rhythmic chirping of crickets in the grass. Let these sounds envelop you, transporting you deeper into a state of inner peace and tranquility.

As you listen, feel the cool, crisp air of the night on your skin, the gentle caress of the breeze brushing against your cheeks and hair. Visualize the twinkling stars overhead—their soft light dancing across the sky like diamonds scattered on velvet. Allow yourself to be captivated by the beauty and serenity of this moment, feeling a sense of connection and awe for the vastness of the universe.

With each breath you take, feel the stillness and quiet of the night filling your lungs, invigorating and energizing you from within. Inhale deeply and breathe in the scent of the mountain air—the aroma of pine and earth, the faint hint of wildflowers carried on the breeze. Let these scents transport you to a place of pure relaxation and bliss.

As you gaze up at the stars, allow yourself to be fully present in this moment of quiet serenity. Notice how the constellations seem to come alive against the backdrop of the night sky, their ancient stories and myths unfolding before your eyes. Feel a sense of wonder and awe wash over you as you contemplate the mysteries of the universe, knowing that you are a part of something greater than yourself.

End ⟶ Know that you can return to this Celestial Observatory whenever you need to find solace and inspiration in the midst of the chaos of daily life. Carry the sense of peace and wonder that you've discovered here with you as you journey forward, knowing that the universe is always there to guide and inspire you.

or

Extend

When you're ready, slowly begin to bring your awareness back to the present moment, gently opening your eyes and taking a few deep breaths. Take a moment to stretch your limbs and wiggle your fingers and toes, feeling the energy flowing freely through your body once more. ∎

As you continue to gaze up at the stars, allow yourself to sink deeper into a state of profound peace and tranquility. Feel the cool, crisp air of the night surrounding you, the gentle rustle of the trees in the breeze. With each breath you take, feel a sense of calm and serenity wash over you, as if you are becoming one with the universe itself.

Now, let's deepen your connection to the cosmos by engaging your senses even further. Close your eyes once more and listen closely to the sounds of the night—the distant hum of insects in the air, the soft murmur of leaves rustling in the wind, the occasional twinkle of a star shooting across the sky. Let these sounds envelop you, transporting you deeper into a state of inner peace and tranquility.

As you listen, feel the cool, crisp air of the night on your skin and the soft caress of the breeze ruffling your hair. Visualize the twinkling stars overhead—their soft light casting a warm glow over the landscape, illuminating the darkness with their ethereal beauty. Allow yourself to be captivated by the beauty and serenity of this moment, feeling a sense of connection and awe for the vastness of the universe.

With each breath you take, feel the energy of the cosmos coursing through your veins, invigorating and energizing you from within. Inhale deeply and breathe in the scent of the night—the aroma of pine and earth, the faint hint of wildflowers carried on the breeze. Let these scents transport you to a place of pure relaxation and bliss.

As you continue to gaze up at the stars, allow yourself to be fully present in this moment of quiet serenity. Notice the uncountable points of light against the backdrop of the night sky and the time it has taken for their light to reach your eyes at this moment. Feel a sense of wonder and awe wash over you as you contemplate the mysteries of the universe, knowing the atoms in your very body were once part of ancient stars themselves.

Know that you can return to this Celestial Observatory whenever you need to find solace and inspiration in the midst of the chaos of daily life. Carry the sense of peace and wonder that you've discovered here with you as you journey forward, knowing that the universe is always there to guide and inspire you.

When you're ready, slowly begin to bring your awareness back to the present moment, gently opening your eyes and taking a few deep breaths. Take a moment to stretch your limbs and wiggle your fingers and toes, feeling the energy flowing freely through your body once more.

Conclusion

Embracing the Journey

As we come to the end of "Journey Into Nature: Guided Meditations for Inner Peace and Relaxation," we reflect on the transformative power of visualization and the profound connection between mind, body, and spirit. Throughout this collection, we have embarked on journeys to serene forests, tranquil lakesides, majestic mountains, and enchanting landscapes, guided by the gentle voice of imagination and the wisdom of nature.

Each guided imagery meditation offered a pathway to relaxation, healing, and self-discovery, inviting us to immerse ourselves in the beauty of the natural world and reconnect with our innermost selves. We have witnessed the play of light and shadow on canyon walls, felt the gentle caress of ocean breeze on our skin, and marveled at the twinkling stars in the night sky—all from the comfort of our own minds.

Guided imagery is more than just a therapeutic technique; it is a journey of exploration and wonder, a reminder of the infinite possibilities that lie within us and around us. Through guided imagery, we have learned to quiet the chatter of the mind, listen to the whispers of the heart, and embrace the present moment with gratitude and openness.

As we close this collection, let us carry the lessons learned and the experiences gained into our daily lives. May we continue to nurture our well-being, cultivate mindfulness, and deepen our connection to the natural world. And may we always remember that the greatest journeys are not measured in miles traveled, but in moments cherished and memories made.

Thank you for joining us on this journey into the heart of nature and the depths of the imagination. May the transformative power of guided imagery continue to illuminate your path and inspire you to live each moment with intention, joy, and a sense of awe and wonder.

Made in the USA
Monee, IL
14 September 2025